Closet Decluttering Workbook

Alaya Aifel

Contents

One

Introduction

I am glad to see that you have opened this workbook!

Let me guess. You don't know where to put your "nothing to wear"?

We all know Narnia, and we know exactly where it is – in our closet, a magical world where you don't know where anything goes or where anything is.

When you're sorting through your wardrobe, how many times do you say, "Oh, what a cute blouse [or skirt, or sandals]! Wow, I completely forgot about this!"? Or, after buying a new item, how often do you remember that somewhere in the depths, on the farthest shelf, the new is the well-forgotten old – now in duplicate?

I have tried very hard to make this workbook as applied and systematized as possible, so that such an incomprehensible notion as "a good wardrobe" can be understood even by those who have never thought about how everything works in the world of clothes.

I hope that by the end of the workbook, you will know the wisdom of taming your wardrobes and will be able to continue managing your closet independently. By the end of the book, you should be able to swing open the door of your closet and feel abundance!

The work is dusty sometimes, but quite exciting. In short, we can do it!

Two

Introductory Briefing

I like theory to be interspersed with practice, so I hope you've read my book *I Will Dress Any Body Type*. If you haven't, though, that's okay – we will rely on your experience, intuition, and taste.

You will assemble your starting seasonal wardrobe according to this strategy: you will sort out your seasonal clothes, distribute the "survivors" into capsules, and make a list of missing things (considering your concept and wardrobe structure). If you wish, you will buy everything you need and be able to wear it immediately.

I strongly advise you not to try to work out your closet all at once. I'll tell you right away, your wardrobe is a hard-to-train beast – you can't take it by surprise. Sort it out season by season. In other words, deal with sorting out, distributing, and making your list of purchases on the eve of a new season or during it. This is easier and more logical because you will have access to the seasonal basic assortment in stores. Additionally, you will get an understanding of trends and may want to refresh your seasonal wardrobe immediately.

All in all, you'll have your entire wardrobe worked out gradually over the course of a year. The first season you work with will be the most difficult one, and the next ones are usually easier to refine.

Wardrobe seasons and calendar seasons

Note that we are talking about wardrobe seasons, not the seasons on the calendar. For example, in your climate area, you might work with three seasons:

Winter (very late fall, winter, and early spring)

Demi-season (mid-autumn and mid-spring)

Summer (end of spring and summer and the very beginning of fall)

But there might be two or four seasons, depending on where you live. The seasonality of your wardrobe is also influenced by your lifestyle and transportation. In some parts of Europe, many people develop only two seasonal wardrobes ("cold" for fall and winter, "warm" for spring and summer), and that it is enough.

Boxes and a rail for the survivors

During the wardrobe sorting phase, you will be dividing garments into five or six groups: "Throw away," "Keep," "Special/Utilitarian items," "Questionable," "Does not suit my lifestyle," and maybe "Divas" and/or "Buffer."

To do this, you will need boxes to put each group in. I also advise you to hang your survivors on a rail (roll-out rack for clothes), because it will be clearer to assess them and finalize your capsules. If you don't have one, that's okay. Just designate a place where your finalists will be.

A full-length mirror and/or a camera phone

When you're trying on clothes to decide what to do with them, it's best if you can see yourself at full height. Therefore, it will be convenient if you have a large mirror or a phone with a camera to take selfies.

Don't be a perfectionist!

In this workbook, I have condensed years of training into less than 100 pages. I want you to absorb 27,000 megabytes at a time. And like Neo from *The Matrix*, you will succeed. I understand that you will get discouraged sometimes, and sometimes you will be annoyed that I'm not going deeper. In those moments, drink some calming tea, meditate, shout into a pillow, do whatever it is that usually brings you back to normal, and don't give up! Do as much as you can, trusting your instincts and taste. Once you build your first capsule, all subsequent ones will be pure play, enjoyment, and development.

Set of mind

How do you usually review your closet? You move things from place to place, get rid of a few things, rediscover long-forgotten purchases. The clutter soon returns, and with it, a sense of dissatisfaction with your appearance. A wardrobe revision is like a surgical procedure. Imagine you're a surgeon. You do not cut out only half of the patient's apendix, saying the other half may be useful. What is going to happen to your patient!? The purpose of the wardrobe revision is to find your hidden capsule. It is already there, trust me.

I would love you to keep in mind the quote by Dalai Lama or Haruki Murakami: "Pain is inevitable. Suffering is optional"

That's all the instructions. I hope you enjoy this program and gain a lot of insight. Let's get started!

Three

Beginning

To start off, you have an introductory assignment to complete. It's extensive, but not complicated! Everything you are going to do now is of real, practical importance.

Catalog your habitual images. Collect and photograph eight to ten (or more) images of your usual looks – how you really walk around every day. Register what you wear using the table below. You should include one or two dressy images (semi-formal or "red carpet" looks), a couple of images with outerwear, and the rest of the everyday images without outerwear (how you dress for work, on weekends, etc.). Your outfits and descriptions should be complete - with shoes and a bag. You can use the self-timer on your phone camera or just take a full-length photo in the mirror.

These photos will help you look objectively at your style habits and analyze your wardrobe in terms of its modernity, color techniques, and sets or formulas. When you finish going through this workbook, meaning you will have created the same catalog with new images, you will compare and see visually the dynamics of your new wardrobe.

I have attached a few modified pages of the "What I Wore Tracker," and I invite you to complete it.

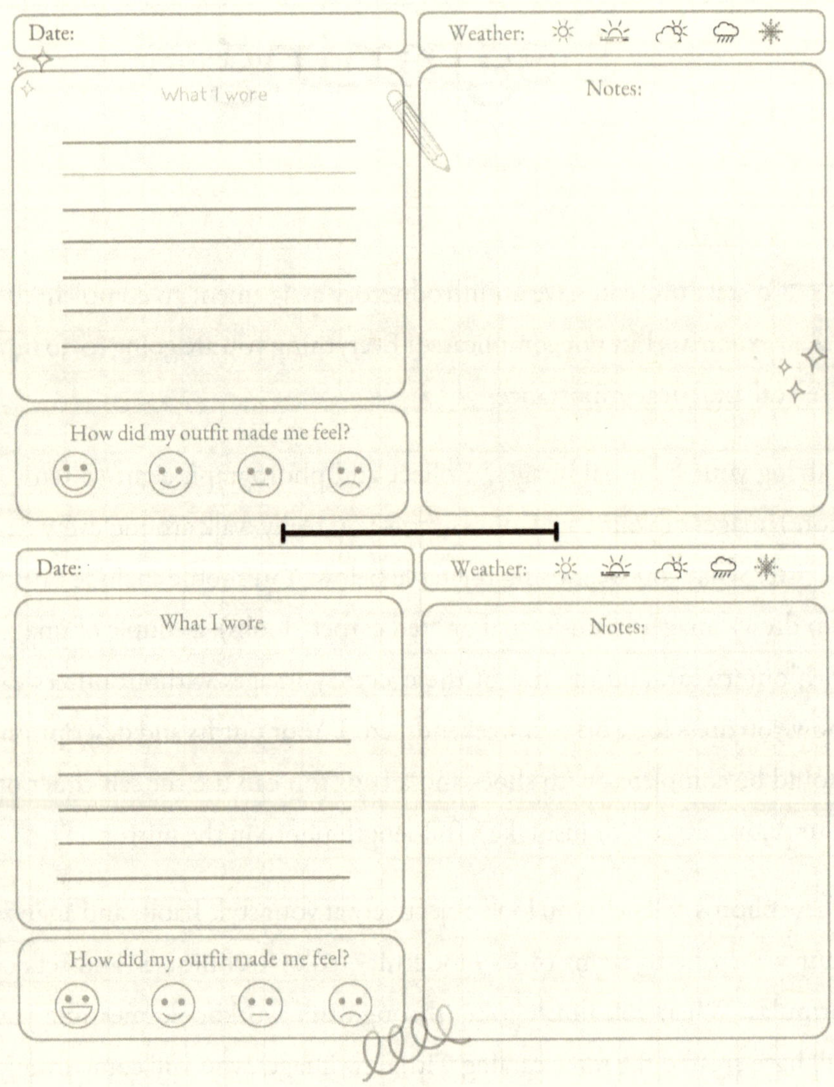

Date:
Weather:
What I wore
Notes:
How did my outfit made me feel?
Date:
Weather:
What I wore
Notes:
How did my outfit made me feel?

Date:

Weather:

What I wore

____
____
____
____
____
____

How did my outfit made me feel?

Notes:

Date:

Weather:

What I wore

____
____
____
____
____
____

How did my outfit made me feel?

Notes:

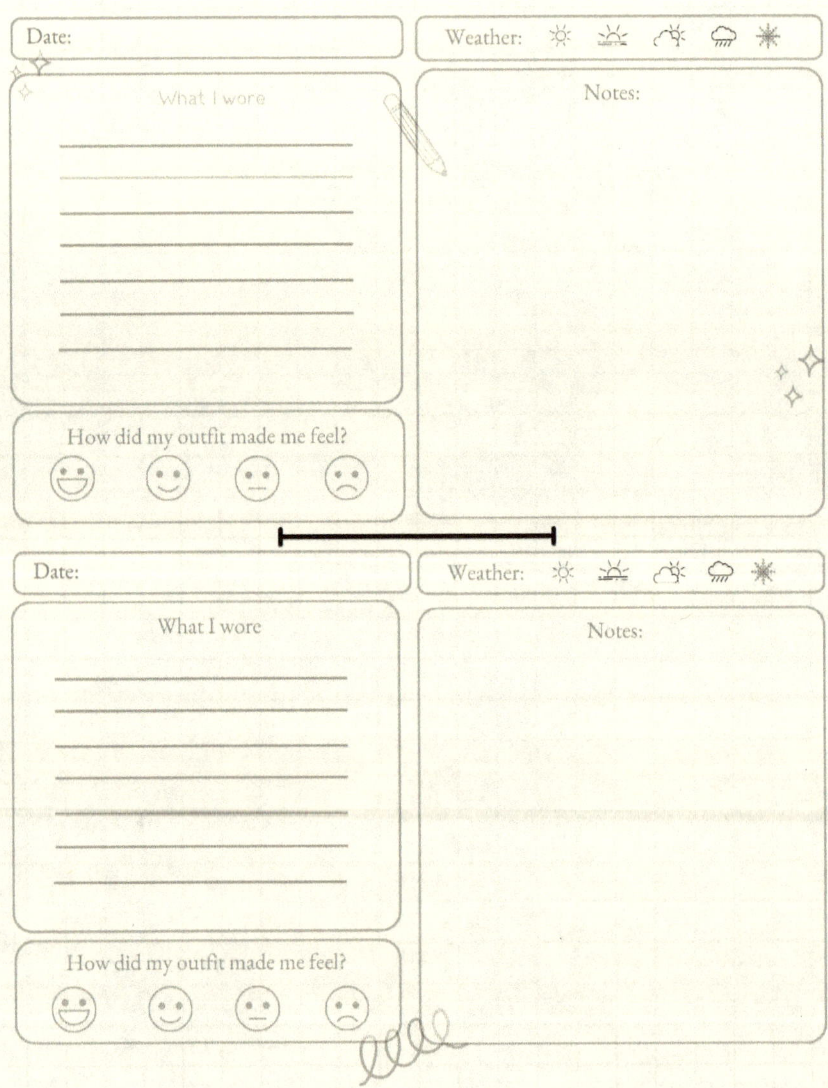
Date:
Weather:
What I wore
Notes:
How did my outfit made me feel?
Date:
Weather:
What I wore
Notes:
How did my outfit made me feel?

Date:

Weather:

What I wore

____

____

____

____

____

____

Notes:

How did my outfit made me feel?

Date:

Weather:

What I wore

____

____

____

____

____

____

Notes:

How did my outfit made me feel?

Four

Me and My Wardrobe

Write a concise essay about yourself and your wardrobe, discussing any issues you'd like to address. I've provided some questions to get you started. Answer briefly or in detail, whichever feels more comfortable.

Where do you live? Does thet transportation you usually use influence the way you dress?

List the areas of your life that require different clothes: work, weekends. sports, tourism; dressy events, other situations that are relevant to you.

Describe briefly the main wardrobe problems that you want to solve and what kind of wardrobe you are striving for (not style preferences, but functional desires - I want a large wardrobe, I want a micro wardrobe, I want capsules for all areas of life, etc.)

What stores do you go to most often?

Problems when choosing and buying clothes?

Formulate how you want to look ideally (here it is about your style preferences and the desired external effect of your image)?

Favorite and not favorite colors, shades, prints. Which ones do you buy and wear more often, and which ones do you want to have in your ideal capsule?

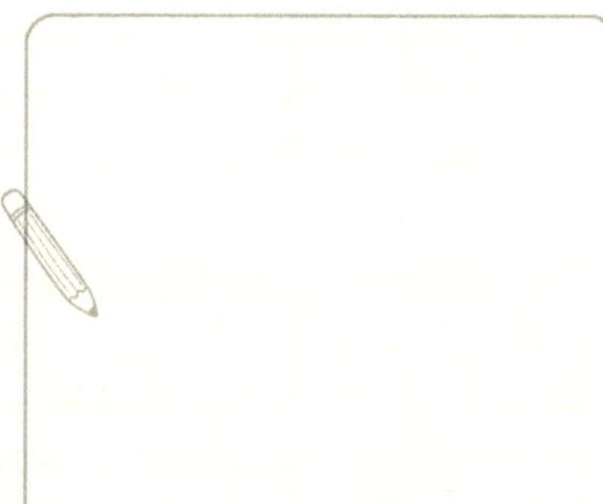

Are there any focal points in your body that you like/don't like to emphasize, want to camouflage, or highlight?

Do you use cosmetics? Would you like to try/change something in that area?

What specific items would you like to incorporate into your wardrobe?
Note that your Wishlist will be corrected gradually during the course.

My Wishlist as of

Five

Analyzing the Real and Desired

You've now documented what you wear most often. Let's assume your favorite formula is "jeans + shirt + cardigan." Go to sites like Farfetch or to the sites for your preferred brands, and find a similar combination that you really like.

Below is a table you can use for this self-reflection exercise. On the left side of the table, you will write about your current outfits, and on the right side, you will write about the desired image that you found online. The explanations for three of your formulas are in the attached tables. I find this exercise very useful, as you might get a lot of insights by comparing the discrepancies.

Formula#1	Your Outfit	The Desired Image
Try to analyze the picture in detail (evaluate separately the color palette on the right and left, the overall mood, key items, fabrics, prints or décor)		
Which of the things you want are already being implemented in your wardrobe? (perhaps you are already using the desired palette or specific accent pieces). Where do you find total discrepancies (this is an important insight, as it will be your main task to change your wardrobe strategy).		

Formula#2	Your Outfit	The Desired Image
Try to analyze the picture in detail (evaluate separately the color palette on the right and left, the overall mood, key items, fabrics, prints or décor)		
Which of the things you want are already being implemented in your wardrobe? (perhaps you are already using the desired palette or specific accent pieces). Where do you find total discrepancies (this is an important insight, as it will be your main task to change your wardrobe strategy).		

Formula#3	Your Outfit	The Desired Image
Try to analyze the picture in detail (evaluate separately the color palette on the right and left, the overall mood, key items, fabrics, prints or décor)		
Which of the things you want are already being implemented in your wardrobe? (perhaps you are already using the desired palette or specific accent pieces). Where do you find total discrepancies (this is an important insight, as it will be your main task to change your wardrobe strategy).		

Updated Wishlist

Now you have a more conscious list of your own style requests, which you can develop further and implement. In the process, you will adjust it many times - but your goals will always be in front of your eyes. I suggest you add to your wish list those techniques or specific things that you are ready to work on. For example, I am ready to expand the color palette, I need to use layering, I may add another bag.

What specific items would you like to incorporate into your wardrobe? Note that your Wishlist will be corrected gradually during the course.

My Wishlist as of

Six

Moodboard

The photos from the stores you worked with in the last step will now become part of your moodboard.

If you have already gotten a lot of insights from the previous exercise and you think it is enough for your development, then you don't need to do this activity. But if it is not enough, your next task is to create a moodboard with images of bloggers, street stylers, and images from catalogs of online stores that reflect your wardrobe philosophy. This moodboard should be filled with pictures that make you scream, "Oh yeah, that's me! I want to look like that!" You can save your collection in your secret board on Pinterest.

A moodboard is your "wish list," and it can be quite chaotic. It can reflect any aspect of the wardrobe theme: imagery, individual items, colors or palettes, hairstyles or makeup. Most often, these are images that you like subconsciously. I hope that in the process, you will understand why you like them (color combinations, style, mood, or something else). You do not have to compare the moodboard with your real parameters or lifestyle! We won't be copying images, but only picking out individual components or designs that will help us get similar effects or moods.

If you're surfing on Pinterest and don't understand where to start or you get the "wrong" pictures, what do you do? Start your search with a specific item or outfit that you like. Type in a search like "jeans trend 202X" or "total gray street style." Or include the name of a style icon you like: "[name] street style 202X." If you indicate the year, the images shown to you will be more relevant, and you can also enter a brand or a specific model ("Celine bag 202X trend"). And then the images are pulled up by themselves (under the open picture, you will see similar images).

Many of us like specific brands with a consistent mood or style (like COS or Everlane) and the images in their catalogs or on Instagram. You can flip through these images, and if you say, "Oh, this is how I would like to dress," save them!

Seven

Wardrobe Review

We're going to review our wardrobe in several rounds.

It is important to sift out clothes that will not be further involved in the formation of your wardrobe because they do not align morally or physically with the role we would like them to play. Clothes that "make it to the semifinals" are not your final wardrobe yet – these are just the garments we've given a chance. The pre-finals will be even tougher because we'll incorporate color concepts and wardrobe aesthetics. As I mentioned above, it's best to start only with the current or upcoming season! It's more convenient, and there is an understanding of the potential of your wardrobe in the context of the season.

Inventories

For some people, making an inventory is a torment, and I totally understand. But on the other hand, statistics are a powerful and objective tool – you can't argue with that. I'm not going to lie, the thought of taking inventory of your closet can be daunting. But it's just a thought. Doing the real work, with the right approach and mindset, can be an absolutely joyful, liberating, and not at all agonizing endeavor.

After filling in the Table of Inventories, you will see an objective picture of what you really have. You'll make small discoveries about yourself and your character, and most importantly, you'll arrive not at the finish line, but at the desired start!

The conclusions you come to can be completely unpredictable, sometimes dramatic. It all depends on your character, experience, and life situation. I'll list a few possibilities:

- Many of you will realize the chaotic nature of your purchases. Yes, we might believe that clothes are something very superficial, not worthy of attention. Out of overconfidence, we shop without a plan. Now the decision has been made – the next shopping list should be worked out.

- Some of you will realize that your closet is poorly organized and re-hang everything in a new way.

- Some of you, after counting the cost of parasites in the closet that don't pay rent in the form of joy, will decide to change your approach fundamentally – build a capsule of minimum items and free up a lot of closet space. That's just great!

- Some will go to a psychologist to remove the emotional addiction to stuff. You've come to the realization that you can't let go, and that feeling is preventing you from taking the next step.

Whatever conclusions you reach, I congratulate you! You are on the right path.

The good news is that you can combine the inventory process with the first round of your first wardrobe review (next chapter), so it will be very quick!

Inventories

Item	How Many	Comments
Top		
T Shirt		
Polo		
Shirt		
Blouse		
Turtleneck		
Sweater		
Skirt		
Pants		
Jeans		
Shorts		
Sundress		
Casual Dress		
Cocktail Dress		

Inventories

Item	How Many	Comments
Waistcoat		
Jacket		
Cardigan		
Pantsuit		
Bomber		
Denim Jacket		
Biker Jacket		
Trench		
Parka		
Short coat		
Coat		
Down jacket		
Fur Coat		
Sandals		

Inventories

Item	How Many	Comments
Pointed Toe Ballet Shoes		
Shoes (Mary Jane, Oxfords ect)		
Loafers		
Sneakers or Keds		
Booties		
Ankle Boots		
Boots		
High Boots or Jackboots		
Shopper bag		
Crossbody Bag		
Bag for work		
Clutch		

Inventories

Item	How Many	Comments
Backpack		
Belt		
Shawl		
Scarf		
Hat		
Fedora Hat		
Earings		
Bracelets		
Necklace		
Ring		
Other		
Other		
Other		
Other		

Eight

First Round: Pre-Selection

This is the easiest round in terms of sorting out. You dump out one group (for example, pants) from the closet and prepare five "boxes" for sorting.

You must work out each garment mechanically, assessing it consistently according to the following parameters:

Physical condition

Size

Whether you like it

Whether it suits your lifestyle

Special/utilitarian use

As you assess each garment, put it into one of the following boxes:

NO – Physically "tired" clothes that cannot be repaired. Clothes that you do not like. Things that are too small for you. We do not keep clothes that deprive us of self-confidence.

SPECIAL/UTILITARIAN – Utilitarian clothes in good condition and size. They might be failing stylistically, but you don't plan to use them in your main wardrobe. I must say there are exceptional closets without such utilitarian items because every situation in life is fundamentally important – sometimes it is not clear whether someone is gardening or posing for Vogue. But in most cases, such clothes are necessary. However, do not turn this box into a warehouse called "pity to throw out!" Sportswear, special clothes or shoes for some hobby of yours, and home clothes go into SPECIAL too.

QUESTIONABLE – Clothes you can do something with, sew on, upgrade. Clothes that are too big for you go either into NO or QUESTIONABLE (only if you are sure that you will revamp them!).

DOES NOT SUIT MY LIFESTYLE – For example, you might be on maternity leave, yet your closet is full of business outfits. Or you may have an impression that you have a lot of great stuff, but you walk around in the same outfit all the time. This box is not for throwing out or giving away. Just remove the clothes that do not fit your lifestyle from your closet.

YES – Garments in good condition, in your size. These go to the semi-finals. Sentimental clothes dear to your heart (jeans from the first year of college, on which you measure your butt every five years) go to YES, provided they still fit you.

What should you do after the first round of cleanup?

Keep the NO box for now – if you've over-cleaned, you may be able to get some stuff back. But most likely, there will be more clothes added there.

The key YES box of good stuff is your main field for further work. Hang them on a separate rail because these garments will have to be sorted out further.

Put the box of SPECIAL/UTILITARIAN clothing somewhere close by. It is very possible that some of the good stuff that did not make it to the finals will go in here.

Keep the QUESTIONABLE box in plain sight. In the process, you will find the answers to your questions and empty it. Some things may come back in line, but the lion's share will go to hell.

P.S. For those who are afraid to get rid of things or are worried that they must clean out a lot, I can say very confidently and authoritatively that building a capsule from scratch is *much* easier than building it from many uncoordinated items.

It is tea time now!

Nine

Second Round: Divas and the Concept of Basic Wardrobe.

At this point, we must learn about the concept of a Basic Wardrobe, then run every item though this filter.

Here's a quote from *Let's Shop in Our Own Closet*:

"What is basic? First and foremost, it is the CUT.

Many people think that we are talking about color and picture things in black and white or maybe in beige and blue. However, the basics don't mean a particular color; they mean the cut and the ability of every item to work with each other. They can be of any color at all!"

So, basic clothes are clothes of any color or print without any décor and of a simple, basic cut. For example, if we're talking about tops, it would be a basic straight shirt, a T-shirt plus a long-sleeved tee, or a blouse: not fitted and with simple necklines (U, V, round, or boatneck), without voluminous sleeves, interesting cuts or perforations, complicated darts, or open backs.

I hope you get the idea. The same requirements apply to outerwear, tops, bottoms, accessories, and shoes.

Styles such as city casual, business casual, and smart casual consist of basic clothes, one hundred percent. Most of us and a huge number of street stylers dress in basic items. At first glance, it seems that the world of clothing is full of variety. In a way, that's true. But try to decolorize the outfits of street stylers and take into account the textures of outfits, and all you have left is a basic modern cut.

So, where I started is where I'll end. The basic wardrobe is not boring at all. You can create super interesting capsules! The only requirement is that clothes have to be of good quality.

This is one of the most important rounds, so please take it seriously.

What are Divas? Capricious things with character, refusing to cooperate with other members of your closet society. Divas are often items with unusual cut or décor.

A capsule wardrobe is a well-coordinated team. As for Divas, you need to create and invest in a separate project. That means separate accessories, shoes, and clothing. If you have many such items, then start another box labeled "Divas." You might also open a separate section in your closet called "Museum."

Divas are the hardest to part with, because they are creative, often designer items. Even if they were bought on sale, they might be high-quality, interesting garments. They are pleasant to look at, but you don't wear them – or you wear them, but not often. Sometimes, these are not designer items in any way; they're just strange clothes with a weird character. You don't understand what style they belong to; they attracted you at the time, but you don't wear them. Over time, they become museum pieces. What's that category? Museum pieces fill your closet, making you feel like you have a lot of good creative stuff, while you still walk around in jeans and a T-shirt and don't understand why you don't like your reflection in the mirror.

What's going to happen to your Divas? I know you're sorry to part with them. So, keep them in the Museum section in the beginning. Check them from time to time, say hello, invite them for solo concerts. Some of you will realize it's time to part with them quite quickly, while some will take a year, maybe even a few years. Some will be prompted by life circumstances, like moving, weight gain, or a spiritual breakthrough. Sooner or later, you will do something with your Divas, give yourself time, but in the meantime, put them in the Museum section. Preferably, keep that section out of your closet. Sentimental stuff like wedding dresses goes out of your closet too. Where? To the Museum section.

A few more words about this Museum section. First, it isn't as bad as it might seem. You buy paintings, posters, figurines, decorative plates, vases. These objects mainly have one function: they're your muses. They inspire you, create coziness, and improve the overall Feng Shui of your home. A Museum section can also inspire you, provided you can afford such a section in terms of space. In addition to your wedding dress and any inherited clothes, expensive or exotic embroidered things that you definitely don't wear and don't know what they could be worn with will be moved there. You will act as the curator of this Museum. I must say that Divas and the Museum items are not entirely the same thing – Divas are often the result of emotional shopping and are easier to part with.

So, as I said, you will work as a museum curator. It seems to me that the main criterion should be your feelings. Ask yourself: "Do these things bring me joy? Do they nourish me?" If you have one feeling – "sorry to throw them out, bought them overpriced" – then embrace them and offer them as gifts.

I hope you've made it to this point and are ready to move on to the next round.

Ten

Third Round: Modernity and Doubles (Extras)

I do not know your temperament or your timetable. You might do all the rounds in one day, or you might extend the process for several days. I would like you to understand that sorting out our wardrobe is not just about throwing stuff away. We learn a lot about ourselves and about clothes in general during the process.

Filter 1: Modernity

Whether clothes are modern or not does not depend on seasonal trends. It is the overall impression of your appearance that counts. This impression is set by global processes and meets the spirit of the times.

Global trends reflect the general mood in society, so they change at a leisurely pace and affect very fundamental characteristics in clothing and appearance:

- styles, lengths, fitting

- general techniques of "what to wear with what"

- color techniques reflecting the general mood

- iconic items reflecting the zeitgeist

- new fabrics

It is on these global points that we check ourselves and our wardrobe for relevance!

I suggest going back to the pictures from the internet that you worked with at the beginning. Remember, I asked you to take your key formulas and compare them with similar pictures from the stores. Notice their fabric, their cut, their fit.

Think of movies or TV series from ten to fifteen years ago (*The Good Wife*, *Suits*, etc.). Take, for example, business style and compare it with modern business looks. Identify the changes that have occurred. You'll probably see that the fitting has changed drastically. What else? Go back further and watch *The Bishop's Wife* (1947). You'll understand what I mean.

It might be difficult to run this filter because some people do not want to change. I know two women who live nearby. One is seventy-four years old and looks like she is sixty, and the other one is sixty years old but looks seventy-four, or even older. The first one is keeping up with the times, while the other one is stuck somewhere in the past... well, in garments that make her look old. This proves that it is not the number of wrinkles that makes you look old. When you see people from afar, you can't see their face well yet, but you can often tell their age. They learned how to dress when they were young and got stuck in that same habit they once developed.

Regardless of which decade you choose to live in, put away clothes made of thin viscose knit, shapeless knitwear, or combined clothes (cotton shirt with knitted back, knitted dress with leather sleeves, etc.) – these combinations are almost always evil, as such garments do not fulfill the function of either sewn clothing or knitwear. One of my tasks here is to talk you out of buying faded, too close-fitting, outdated, weak, or weight-adding clothes. However hard you work on colors or proportions, if your closet is full of clothes like that, no good will come of it. Unfortunately, every brand, from expensive to affordable, still offers out-of-date fashions.

Remove garments with décor, which often cheapens the appearance of clothes. Usually this is found in the inexpensive segment of the market: pearls (on knitwear), large metal buttons (on knitwear, coats, jackets), sequins and rhinestones on knitwear, lace trim on denim.

My advice for shopping in budget brands is to choose clothes that are either completely simple in appearance or have only one accent (either color, or texture, or décor – but not all at once). As a rule, they look more expensive and there is less chance of running into potential faults. The more complicated a garment is externally, the cheaper the execution of all its "decorations" usually is.

Remember, fabric and a semi-fitted cut are the major answer to all your style problems!

Filter 2: Weak doubles (extras)

When you did your inventories, you might have found a lot of doubles and extras.

What are doubles and extras? I will quote myself again:

"There are obvious doubles, such as same-style tees in slightly differing colors, or several pairs of the same type of jeans. You decide what to do with them. As you build your capsule, you will figure out what should be included in it and what shouldn't.

There are also color doubles, implicit ones. Pay attention now! For example, you may have straight gray pants and straight gray jeans. You can argue with that and say that jeans and pants are as different as chalk and cheese. However, an outsider only sees a gray blob at the bottom. It's not really important whether they see pants or jeans. If you have truly decided to go for reducing your wardrobe and increasing its versatility, you won't get anywhere without color. We'll talk about color a lot.

In addition to doubles, there are extras. In movies, they are actors who perform in nonspeaking roles. Let's take a sweater, for example. Let's say you have several. There is your favorite, the dark blue one, which is the main character, and then there are doubles and extras. The extra sweater is not an exact copy of your favorite one. So, it is not quite a double, nor is it a color double because it's green. It doesn't play that much of a role though; all it does is substitute for the blue sweater while it's in the laundry. The extra sweater doesn't go with much of anything except jeans and doesn't bring you all that much joy; you bear with it because needs must. As soon as the blue sweater has had its rest and has been refreshed it goes right back to work because nothing can ever be a match for the prima donna.

Extras or stars-in-reserve can be more or less talented. You are the company director. It's your decision whom to fire and whom to keep."

How do you understand the difference between a strong double and a weak double? It is very simple. You wear strong doubles often, because they fit well and fit into your wardrobe in other ways. If there are reasons why you don't wear something often, it's a weak double. For example, you have five pairs of jeans, but two pairs are a little tight, or they have buttons and your body does not like buttons. These two pairs of jeans with buttons are good quality jeans that look new (of course they do – you never wear them), so your mind says you shouldn't put them away, but what does your body say?

Strong doubles will go to the semifinals, while some of your weak doubles might migrate to the SPECIAL/UTILITARIAN box.

Now you will have to write down what is hanging on the rail. Congratulations, you've made it to the semifinals!

Semi-Finals

Item	How Many	Comments

Semi-Finals

Item	How Many	Comments

Eleven

Round Four: Your Body Type

Now you have the semifinalists hanging on the rail, and you have your wish list of purchases. Some of you already have a clear idea of what you need to buy, and some of you are still halfway there. Wherever you are, let's analyze your wish list. How does it work with what's hanging on the rack? Most importantly, do the items on the rail and on your list help you dress your body?

Unfortunately, I can't embed the entire book *I Will Dress Any Body Type* here, but I can offer questions and tips that will help you out.

1 What type of body do you have?

Triangle (also known as Pear or Low)

Hourglass

Rectangle

Upper Body Type (Apple and Inverted Triangle)

2 What individual features does your body have?

Many people consider individual features of their body as their main advantages, while others, for various reasons, feel bad about them. Underline what applies to you.

Full ankles

Wide hips

A bit of a belly

Big breasts

Full arms

Short neck

Slouching

Petite

Other

3 What are your general tactics for dressing your body, taking into consideration your body type and its individual features?

Here are several ideas:

Working with necklines, for example, a V neckline for inverted triangle, or big breasts or crew neck for triangles

Creating soft verticals by using monochrome outfits, layering (leaving your cardigan or jacket open), vertical prints, hills, floor-length pants

Concentrating on tops to take attention away from your bottoms

Concentrating on bottoms to take attention away from your tops

Focusing on your shoulder line, e.g., when you are slouching

4 List of items for key body types from *Let's Shop in Our Own Closet*

"I have a hunch that everyone knows about their silhouettes. Or is this the professional tunnel vision acting up? There are clear types, but life is stronger than any categorizing. You thought you were "nearly a triangle," but once you gave birth, you've got a strangely mixed-up figure…

The Theory of Body Types does work. It simply works with a single parameter – the volume at the top and at the bottom. We are well aware that there can be two women with the Inverted Triangle body type where one has a long neck and the other has a short one, one has a short torso and the other has a long one, one has a flat belly and the other does not. These are the nuances that the Theory of Body Types does not address.

If you are interested, here is a list of items for key body types. It's best if you look through this list with interest rather than awe – it is not the Criminal Code, after all. You may and should break the rules. If you're not interested, just skip to the next chapter.

INVERTED TRIANGLE

Is your body the inverted triangle shape? Then we're looking for a list of the following items. Make sure you write this down – there's no fluff here.

In this case, the most interesting things happen at the bottom. For example, you have thrilling boots, then a small patch of bare skin, then amazing leggings, and you can cover up everything on top. You can use tops that flare out, tops with raglan sleeves, with a V or U neck or a halter neck.

You can go and Google Demi Moore; she demonstrates all this wonderfully. All her tops are monochrome and minimalistic with no ruffles, frills, or decorations, whereas her jeans are stone-washed, ripped, or embroidered. You can wear flared or relaxed-fit pants, bright-colored or with prints. They should have a low waist. They can be baggy. Watch the movie *Ghost*. Now for the skirts. They should have a low waist and be wraparound, trapeze, or pleated; tulip skirts are also great. Jackets should go down to the hips and should be single-breasted; oversized ones work too. You should have A-line overcoats, straight single-breasted coats with a V neck, oversized or egg-shaped ones.

RUBENESQUE

Are you a Rubenesque woman? Then you need fewer decorations, ruffles, or pleats. You should not bustle and create an event; you are a beautiful event in your own right. You should not have to speak, but quietly place your sumptuous body above elegant shoes. Pumps with a square throat are a great option.

Loose tunics, wrap dresses, and bottom-flaring shirt dresses are just right for you. You should wear plunging necklines and embroidered necks that remind us of times long gone. Wear flowing skirts, trapeze skirts, or straight ones. Loose knitted pants, evenly colored jeans, pants with a low waist, and straight ones with wide legs all work for you. You have no need for all those holes, washed denim, or cargo pockets. On the other hand, an Empire line dress with a very high waist or a long dress with a plunging neckline would be just right. You can play at the 1920s, when the waist was worn low. Coats should be trapeze, A-line, or egg-shaped. There's no need to button your coat. Stylists say that this creates a vertical line, but all I see is Saskia, Rembrandt's wife, in the nude. There is so much love in that painting! Invest in accents and accessories. They'll suit you better than anyone else. Get rich purses and bracelets. Your story is all about luxury.

TRIANGLE

Is your body shape a triangle (they say this is the most common type)? That means we focus at the top. You can use everything: hairstyle, earrings, scarves, puffed sleeves, tops with interesting collars or a round or square neckline, or even off-the-shoulder ones. The bottoms should be mid-waist or high-waist. Pants can be flared, palazzo, bootcut, or straight. Wear midi skirts. Wear bomber jackets and straight or A-line coats. Egg-shaped coats are great too. This is not an exhaustive list, just the basic one.

HOURGLASS

We won't discuss the hourglass body shape. I think it's rather obvious.

Everything I am telling you here is based on classical principles of harmony. That's when we try to balance the top and bottom in triangle or inverted triangle body types or when we want to pinpoint a waist in a rectangle body type. In essence, we aim towards creating the hourglass silhouette. That's what pleases our eye the most. You can play with silhouettes and deliberately break up the usual proportions, but that is not what we are talking about here.

So, if you have the hourglass body type, you would have to try very hard if you really wanted to ruin your natural silhouette.

RECTANGLE

Do you have a rectangle body shape? Then you should wear tops with voluminous sleeves or strapless ones. Wear halter necks. It is better to look at Gwyneth Paltrow many times than to read about her as many times. Wear tops with ruffles, decorated or with prints on the chest and shoulders. Wear T-shirts or blouses with deep, square, or round necklines.

Generally, a woman with this type of body shape can create volume wherever she wants to attract attention. Bottoms should have a low waist, but there are a lot of exceptions. You can wear A-line skirts, as well as semi-circle or wraparound ones. Wear slouchy, bootcut, wide-legged, culotte, or flared pants. You can have pockets in your jeans that everyone else is banned from because they widen the hips. You should wear dresses with a plunging neckline or an open back, as well as high-waist dresses, A-line ones, kaftans, and kimonos.

You can wear off-the-shoulder dresses. It is better to wear single-breasted jackets than double-breasted ones and to wear A-line, egg-shaped, or oversized coats, as well as single-breasted straight ones and bomber jackets.

Let's finish up with the dry official stuff.

APPLE

With the apple-shaped body type, it is a little difficult to give universal advice. Apple-shaped bodies are so varied, as are the other types. You should wear loose and straight tops and blouses with a V or U neck to enhance the portrait zone. You can also wear loose, long tunics and blouses or any tops with an asymmetrical hem and three-quarter-length sleeves. You can also wear trapeze, circle, semi-circle, or wraparound skirts, and maybe even mini-skirts. It is better if your pants have a side fly. Wear dresses with a low waist in the 1920s style. You can also wear A-line, high-waist, asymmetrical hem, floor-length, and plunging-neck dresses, or shirt dresses. Your coats and jackets should be single-breasted, straight, or A-line, or you can wear oversized and egg-shaped ones."

Assignment: Write down your current strategies for dressing your body. Do clothes on your rail and in your wish list help you in your strategies?

What new things would you like to try? Describe your three or four formulas that work best for you and draw them.

"For example, one woman who was a CEO found this combination to wear to work: a pair of pants and a blouse with a round neck and no turn-back collar (it was just great that she got rid of the collar!). When she was in her office, she wore sneakers and her jacket hung on the back of a chair. If she had to go out to a meeting and impress someone, she would put on the jacket (that acts as masculine armor nowadays), wear high heels to scare them even more, and march into battle.

My two most common silhouettes are pants and a sweatshirt or a short top with a midi skirt. You'd think that's just about as dull as ditch water... Not at all! I still can't get over how versatile these seemingly boring silhouettes are."

General tactics of dressing my body taking into consideration my type of body and its individual features.

My Key Formulas

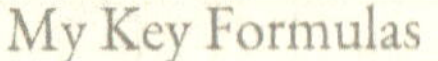

What specific items would you like to incorporate into your wardrobe?
Note that your Wishlist will be corrected gradually during the course.

My Wishlist as of

Twelve

Round Five: Color Palette

Color is such a complex topic that I didn't know how to approach it at first. I'll use an example to give you an idea of how deep you can delve into this. There are four derivatives of your eye color, and each derivative can be expressed in several shades. Really, you could write volumes about colors.

I've decided to be extremely pragmatic. After all, my goal is to give you practical working tips – life hacks, if you will – that will help you figure out how to put together a color scheme for your capsule.

Color is a pretty strong filter. Many good semifinalists may not make it to the finals. What should you do with them? Keep them. They can do spot work. In some companies, there's permanent staff and then there's freelancers. Your pieces that did not pass the color exam will be those freelancers. You keep them but take them away from the rail of finalists. First and foremost, however, you must hire permanent staff, since your goal is to create your main capsule.

How do you pick the right colors for your closet?

Essentially, to understand the myriad of shades and capture the essence, you need to study colors and how they behave. For example, figure out why there are so many different blues or purples, and which blue is yours. Then you must understand your appearance, because we are a complex patch of color, and then find out which of the thousands of shades offered by nature and modern industry, as well as prints, are right for you.

This process is like the study of a diverse range of cuts and all the features of your own body, ending with the choice of certain clothes from the ocean of variety.

The algorithm of actions seems to be clear. But life intervenes in the form of your character and the goals you pursue. Believe me, people's goals can be very different. The difficulty of explaining colors is that we have a lot of starting positions and points.

- Some of you will want to clear out your closet and breathe a sigh of relief. The very fact that you've sorted through the jungle and figured out what you wear is a huge step in saving your budget and managing your life. So, for you, it's not so important to find your individual color yet – the main thing is that everything goes together;

- Some of you love achromats, and don't really care about whether black, white, and gray suit you or not. So, you don't mind reading about color, but you're not going to give up your favorite black.

- Some of you may like fast fashion and fast-paced experimentation. What does that mean in terms of building a capsule? It means that you experiment with colors and if they don't quite suit you, you use makeup or sunglasses to correct excessive contrast, for example. You are often busy clearing out your closet and buying new things. You're on the quest or like to experiment, and that's okay. When choosing a color scheme, you don't base it on your appearance, but on the color combinations you like, regardless of whether they suit your appearance or not.

- Some of us are in an emotional slump. In such periods, we often go to a hairdresser, go on a trip, or change our image with clothes. You want to change your life somehow. The soul screams and asks for a lot of pink and red and a new bag.

- Some would like to approach this issue thoroughly but do not have the resources. By "resources," I mean time and energy first of all.

- And most of you are guided by pragmatism – you have things that have already been bought, they are high-quality and good, and you are not going to give them to anyone. Color-wise, they seem to suit you. Yes, there's chaos, but you can still let them participate in building the capsule. And then there's your budget.

Basically, I'm in favor of the intuitive method. I watch people in stores and see that most of them reach for their colors. You must agree that we are always looking for ourselves, whether it's in choosing a partner, a painting, or furniture design.

I will list the basic color schemes, and if you like any of them, you can apply it to your capsule.

1 Achromats

Let's start with the absence of color – with black, white, and gray. A great many people like to dress in these colors, which are called achromats. We know that black, white, and gray go well together, and the combinations can be divine. You can create calm, elegant looks, as well as ones that are bold and contrasting. You can play with textures and shades. Your capsule can be made up entirely of achromats and be stunning.

2 Conditional achromats

Conditional achromats are colors that can substitute for achromats. Black substitutes are strongly darkened colors, such as very dark blue, green, or burgundy, that appear black in dim light. Conditional achromats also include white substitutes – strongly bleached shades of almost all colors. These are the lightest colors in your palette. Clothes in conditional achromats can be mixed with achromatic clothes (black, white, and gray) – it is up to you. I recommend conditional achromats to those who feel that black is not their color.

3 Adding one color

We're going to get a little more complicated by adding one color to a palette of achromats or conditional achromats. That color can be present in one thing – for example, adding a bright green bag to a black and white combination – or it can be several things of the same color. And the same color can be of different saturation – it doesn't have to be exactly the same. For example, you could have a pink scarf and a more saturated, almost red bag. Or, as in the picture below, you could combine a brightly colored blue scarf, a striped shirt, and a light blue sweater. It's all different shades of blue. They look interesting, and not only because of the difference in shades. The difference in textures plays a big role too.

4 Monochrome looks

Imagine a rainbow made up of pure pigments. Take any color – let's use blue – and dilute it with water, then keep going. Stretch the color from pure pigment to light blue. You can take a light blue blouse and a bag of about the same shade, dark blue jeans, and shoes, and you will get an interesting monochrome look. You can add achromats and conditional achromats to it. Sometimes I hear people ask, "How many colors should be in my palette?" The answer is that one can be enough. In that case, you play with texture and the results will be astonishing.

5 Analogous combinations

Picture the rainbow once again. Combinations of colors that are next to each other are called analogous combinations – for example, purple and blue, or red and orange.

6 Complementary or contrasting combinations

The most daring can choose complementary or contrasting combinations – for example, green/red, yellow/purple, or blue/orange.

7 Triads

To explain triads, I'm going to have to bring up Itten's color wheel. I'm sure you've already seen it, since the internet is saturated with them. In case you haven't, do a search for "Color Circle." The combination of three colors that are equidistant from each other on the color wheel and visually form an equilateral triangle is a triad. Together these colors create a bright palette, so it is important to balance them correctly. To achieve harmony in the triad, take one color for the main and use the other two for accents. This could be red, blue, and green.

Regardless of what you chose, you can build capsules by matching colors by saturation. If you think that contrasting combinations, such as blue and yellow, are only for the brave, I'll try to dissuade you. Try lowering the saturation – then such combinations will not look parrot-like, and you will not look like a national flag. You can achieve a noble and elegant effect.

You can choose colors of the same temperature: only cool colors or only warm colors. Colors with a predominance of yellow and red (the color of fire and sun) are considered warm. Shades where the leading color is blue (water) are called cold. If a color consists of equal amounts of warm and cold, such as green, it is neutral. This "temperature" method of palette selection is suitable for those who clearly understand their skin tone. If you know that cool shades suit you, then go for it. But many of us have a neutral skin temperature, so we shouldn't take this method into consideration.

Enough of the theory. Follow your instincts. The good news is that we are going to build a mini capsule of five to twenty pieces, and I'm sure you can manage this number.

To those who are annoyed and yelling, "How am I supposed to pick colors if I don't know what I need in a capsule? I still don't understand what it is!" my answer is, "Go down below, read chapters 15 through 19, and come back here. I'm waiting for you."

How do you reflect your style goals in a color scheme? Use colors to translate a certain character or effect you want in your looks.

Example #1: I want a more feminine closet. I want to look more delicate and graceful.

The most effective way to do this is to expand into pastels and shades of medium saturation or softer. It's not the pink color, but rather the delicacy and sometimes dustiness that stylistically sets femininity. Any soft combinations of such shades multiply the feminine charisma. This works especially if you choose pro-masculine or unisex things in such shades (pantsuit, knitted sweater, and a concise, geometrically shaped bag).

An old but effective way is to deliberately introduce floral, plant prints or polka dots into your wardrobe. Pearlescent shades also work perfectly.

Example #2: I want to look creative/unusual/spectacular.

Color accents work for such effects. Most of your wardrobe can be concise and plain, and accent pieces can be bright with laconic or complex architectural cuts. Prints work similarly – choose complex geometrics, art, or intricate floral prints.

Example #3: I want to look tougher and stricter.

Contrasts (any kind) and total looks work great for this case. That is, they too should be pre-programmed in a color scheme. I would introduce contrast to monochrome images with the help of accent glasses, lipstick, or bag/shoes – preferably just one element in the image. Metal works well, such as a bag with metal details.

Example #4: I want to look as relaxed and soft as possible. I need a very cozy wardrobe.

This is approximately the same scheme as for adding femininity to the closet. The only difference is that monochromes and soft combinations can be made not only in a light palette, but in any palette up to medium-dark. It is important that the range of contrast in your closet is lower so that all combinations will be as soft and cozy as possible. Fabrics (matte, fluffy, rough) will also play their role. And another technique is accents without the help of bright colors – we work with accent texture on very basic shades.

Assignment: I have attached a template for your palette. Write and think about your capsule color palette. For now, these are just sketches. It will be finalized when we draw the capsule.

A little comment about prints and accents: Your prints should consist of the same colors you use in your capsule. Then not only will you have harmony, but you'll have beautiful, unintentional matchy-matchy, monochrome, and other current color techniques all by themselves.

If you have some favorite printed clothes that are likely to participate in the formation of your capsule, you can now use all the shades from these prints. This will be a good clue for the color scheme.

Prints are selected according to your constitution: the more petite you are, the more petite your prints will be (from medium to small). The taller and larger you are, the larger prints you can use. At plus size, I recommend working with chaotic angular prints, because they add sharpness and diagonals, which better shape the image visually: polka-dot, plant prints, thin stripes, diagonal stripes and rhombuses, abstract prints.

Finally, please keep in mind that accent does not necessarily mean something bright and complicated in cut.

Color Palette of My Capsule

Light Colors				
Medium/Neutral Colors				
Dark Colors				
Prints and Texture				
Metals				

Color Palette of My Capsule

Color Palette of My Capsule

Thirteen

Round Six: Style Concept

We have already started talking about your style concept in the previous chapter, so let's continue.

Whether we like it or not, our clothes can tell others a lot about us, and it's good when our clothes say what we want them to say. How do we express ourselves through the language of clothing? It's lines, color (prints), and texture.

Let's take the example of two sweaters. The first one is linear and graphic. If you complement it with a business suit, it makes a great ensemble. The suit is medieval armor, only in a modern version. Businesswear is a pro-masculine trend with clean lines, angles, smooth surfaces, and, if need be, strong punches of color. Straight lines are the walls we put up between ourselves and other people. We need those lines to create personal boundaries, to play a role, to create detachment.

Take another sweater with a rounded neckline and soft fluffy texture, in beige or pink. If you're wearing it, people want to cuddle you.

It is just two pieces of knitwear, but what a different impression you can make with each one.

So, we have three tools of equal strength: line, color, and texture.

Now you will need to characterize the photos that you took in the beginning. In other words, you need to define your style – the style that you already have. Not what you've saved in your moodboard, but the style for your current lifestyle. This is important! Three adjectives will suffice. Chances are you won't have a drastic style change, but an improvement of what you already have. And all we're doing is upgrading what you already have. The changes can be significant, but within reasonable limits.

I'll say right off the top that I'm not in favor of a dramatic image change. A total restyling can end badly, with a fallback to what you already had. Sometimes it's like jumping from first grade to sixth grade. The jump itself gives a lot of adrenaline, but the subsequent life in not-quite-comfortable surroundings is depressing. I don't mean cases where you move and have a drastic change of climate, or you've been staying at home for seven years with kids and now you get a job with an official dress code.

All in all, move according to your desires and budget, and be adequate!

So, ask yourself: "What impression do I want to make?" We don't need a list of eighteen adjectives. Two or three words will suffice.

It could go something like this:

"Delicate, feminine, elegant."

"Comfortable, cozy, sporty."

"Minimalist, natural."

The first option can be expressed through color, such as beige, pink, or all pastels, or through fabrics like cashmere and silk. Most likely these will be neutral cut pieces with no strongly pronounced angles. As for texture, it will most likely be smooth.

The second option can be expressed through looser, more comfortable fabrics like jersey or knit, as well as through sporty items. And even a business suit can be more relaxing.

The third variant will be expressed through the clarity and brevity of lines. The image will be more silhouetted, with colors close to natural, such as beige, light olive, or stone.

In any field, you can express yourself in different ways. Look at how these suits express different moods.

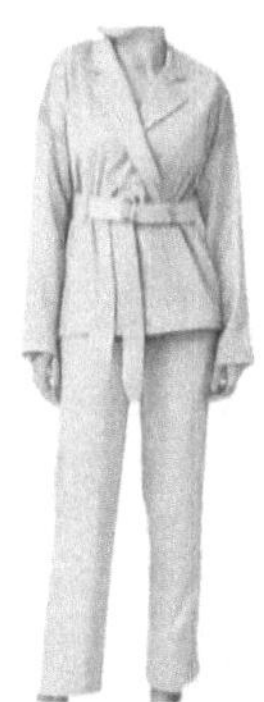  

You may express whatever you want using basic items. I would like to ask you to suspend your quest to be non-boring by introducing strange things into your wardrobe. There is a danger of going overboard. Try to play within the confines of a basic wardrobe. Play with lines, color and print, and textures. For example, the difference in textures will help you create very interesting looks, even if you have your entire capsule in only one color. Play on contrasts: festive and casual (velvet and denim), heavy and light (leather and lace), matte and glossy (knitwear and patent leather), smooth and pronounced textures (smooth pants and noticeable knitting on top).

Let's draft the style concept of your wardrobe.

By now, you have your own "formula," according to which you will continue to choose items in your capsule. When you choose a garment, always answer this question: "Can it give me the effect I want to get?" If yes, then take it. If not, then to hell with it.

In order to create a visual reference, pick up a few conceptualized images. You can find them in your moodboard or on sites for online stores, or you can make collages yourself. There should be three images: "I'm casual," "I'm formal," and "I'm going out."

Sometimes, but not always, working on your concept takes a lot of independent work on the edge of creativity and hard analysis.

Once you are done with the concept and have visualized your style strategy, you can go back to your closet and do a final clean-rail reassessment. Don't forget to review your NO and QUESTIONABLE boxes so that you can finally decide the fate of controversial items with a full understanding of the case.

Now you will be able to remove items that are superfluous in style or accents – garments that no longer fit into your wardrobe and won't be able to provide you with the effects in the looks you want to achieve.

Before you move on to the next chapter, do a little check-up of what you've already done. We'll continue assembling your wardrobe, get into its structure, and fill it with clothes. By that point, you should have a completely sorted out seasonal wardrobe with a color scheme and style concept. If everything is ready, I'm waiting for you in the next chapter!

My Style Concept

Color palette:

My style techniques:

Accents:

Beauty tips, if needed:

My Style Concept

What specific items would you like to incorporate into your wardrobe? Note that your Wishlist will be corrected gradually during the course.

My Wishlist as of

Fourteen

How Many Items Should be in my Wardrobe?

Let's calculate how many items you need for a period of ninety days. Let's say it's for a cold season. To do this, we will make the following assumptions:

1 You want to wear one item once a week. For example, you have green pants, and you will wear them thirteen times in a ninety-day period. Why thirteen? Because ninety days is about thirteen weeks, and you only want to wear your green pants once a week.

2 You will wear three things a day, not counting shoes or outerwear. For example, a pair of jeans, a long-sleeve shirt, and a cardigan. Sometimes it might be a dress, in which case it turns out you only have one thing a day. So, my assumption of three things a day is pretty generous.

3 You only wear one set of clothes a day. I understand that when you're invited to a party, you change your outfit, but for the actual calculation, I didn't take that into account.

With the above assumptions, you need twenty-one items for ninety days, not including shoes or outerwear.

In fact, this equals one week's clothing (3 x 7 = 21). You can repeat that week like Groundhog Day, wearing made-up combinations, or you can juggle twenty-one versatile items. Believe me, you can create a huge number of combinations out of twenty-one items.

Some might take that figure as a guideline, and some will need a lot less. I can tell you that from twelve quality things (including outerwear, shoes, and bag), you can build a super capsule.

Fifteen

Capsules

I won't get tired of repeating this: the most comfortable and compact method of building a wardrobe is to develop it with a capsule system.

A capsule is a minimal set of clothes that match each other in color and style – items that can dress you head to toe in a certain season for certain dressing situations. The good thing about this system is that you don't have unnecessary clothes in your closet or items that are inappropriate for your lifestyle. You always have something to wear and, hopefully, you like what you wear.

There are different types of capsules. Certain pieces can move from capsule to capsule. There are capsules that are relatively closed and self-contained. For instance, if you work as an Entertainer at children's parties, the professional capsule would be self-contained and closed.

The structure of capsules for a certain season can look like this (the size of the circles represents the amount of time a particular area of your life takes up):

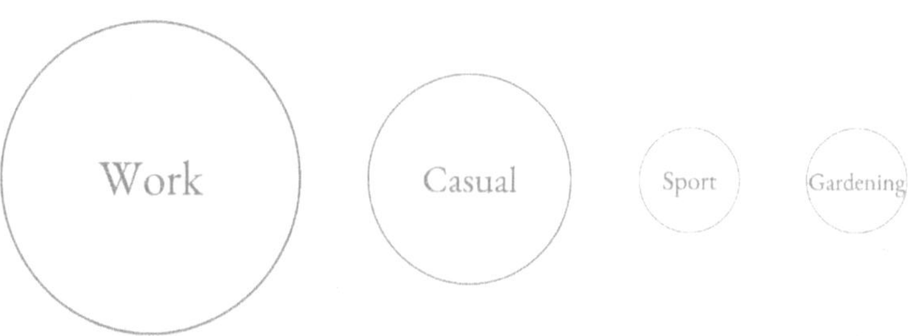

or like this:

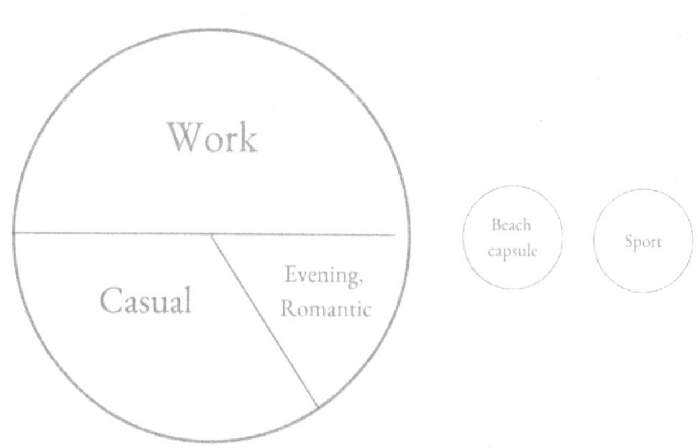

The most compact variant is one main capsule providing for formal, semi-formal, and relaxed situations; for example, you can develop one capsule for all situations plus an off-season mini capsule like "Sports." Your capsules will interact with each other, and some pieces will work in multiple capsules and flow from season to season. For example, jeans, bags, and sneakers roam from season to season.

Assignment:

Let's draw the structure of your wardrobe for the season you are working in. Here is a plan for accomplishing this task:

1 We have already tackled this at the beginning of this workbook, so you may come back to your notes, or do the same thing again only more consciously. Write down all wardrobe situations that are relevant to you, in priority order. Example:

- taking my child for a walk every day

- shopping

- traveling to the office three times a week to meet with clients

- going out once a week to visit or meet my friends in a cafe/restaurant

- going out to a theater/presentation once a month

- hiking once a month

2 Now write down which situations from your list can be covered by one set of clothes. It is important that all situations are "anchored" to a certain capsule. As a result, you will have a list of necessary capsules, which you will develop. You can draw circles or rectangles, or you can draft lists – do as you wish.

Note that micro wardrobes are often developed with just one capsule.

The most common scenario is a wardrobe consisting of these capsules:

- a formal capsule

- a semi-formal capsule – often this is not a separate capsule, but a formal capsule and a few pronounced dressy things to create "evening" looks of different degrees of dressiness

- a comfortable casual capsule that includes active situations such as travel or flights

- "closed" capsules you need – these are often off seasons (home, going to the sea, sports, etc.)

My Capsules

My Capsules

Sixteen

Capsules Continuation

A capsule consists of a base, doubles, and accents.

The base is the backbone, consisting of up-to-date, great clothes. The base dresses you with at least one outfit for any situation.

Doubles are necessary, but they make wardrobes bloated. Be very careful with this category! You have already sorted out your closet and realized that you can have six pairs of jeans, but only one pair is the strongest. Ardent minimalists can do without doubles; having just the backbone will be enough for them.

Accents and trends allow you to diversify your closet. The most important thing is not to overplay. The main rule: buy with an eye on the color palette and the general mood that you want to broadcast. Accents should fit into the base and combine with it.

Accents can be Divas; such accents do not have to be compatible with the whole team but should be completed from the base. But a capsule can do without Divas! Accents can be basic things made in an interesting texture, for example, leather shorts or on-trend basic sneakers. In this case, they will be combined with all the items in the capsule.

Accents can be personal or on trend. For example, you might love leopard print and not care if if it's on trend or not – you adore it regardless of fashion, and it's always with you. Or you love fun socks, and you always wear them. If you like to be fashionable, you can choose basic trending pieces that you like as accent pieces. Otherwise, reveal your personal story as we have already discussed.

The final composition and number of items in the base depends on you. But here's how to check yourself: "Do I have anything to put on for formal/business occasions, romantic/dressy events, and relaxed/casual situations?" This means that each position (top, bottom, and so on) is viewed through the prism of these situations.

If you're building one capsule for all occasions, start with the bottom: for example, jeans for relaxed outings and a skirt for more formal ones. If you're a top-notch minimalist, then have one bottom that covers all occasions. Jeans are unlikely to do the trick unless they are evenly colored, so let it be pants. You can wear them to an exhibition and for leisurely walks. The more compact the closet, the more such universal soldiers there should be.

The versatility of basic clothes is quite a critical principle; it is difficult to put together a compact wardrobe without them. A big part of your capsules should be versatile items that can work in different wardrobe situations. For example, you can wear a jacket to the office, out for a walk with jeans and sneakers, and to a party with a linen skirt.

If you have several capsules planned, let most of the clothes be versatile pieces that can work for multiple capsules at once. This really helps keep your wardrobe from bloating.

Here's an example of a capsule consisting of three sets: relaxed, formal, and semi-formal. Look at it as an idea. Let's break this idea down, and I think you won't have any more questions after that.

Category #1: Casual bottom

Jeans work well for informal looks and even parties. If your style direction is relaxed, jeans with scuffs, blue or gray, will fit well into your capsule. Ripped edges and aged jeans also give jeans a casual look. This is not bad at all if it suits your style. If, however, you're looking to use jeans for a wider range of situations – parties, cocktails, work, everyday casual situations – then choose jeans that are evenly colored. These can be navy blue, black, white, or beige jeans. You can also aim for this choice if "more casual" jeans just don't appeal to you.

Some people do not like jeans – what do they do? Shorts, pants, and skirts made of non-dressy material (cotton, jersey, linen) can be a substitute. For example, knitted pants have gained popularity.

Category #2: Formal bottom

Skirt, pants, culottes – this is the position that is responsible for more formal looks. Usually, these are items that belong to the category of versatile clothes. In principle, if you want to have as few bottoms as possible, it is not necessary to have jeans. The fabric in this case should be dense, for example, fabrics used for suits, but not denim or linen. The styles of pants and skirts should suit your body type. If you have a style with a bias on the bold, brutal side, or if you strive for Romanticism, then you can consider bottoms in leather or satin fabrics. Garments made of such fabrics combine well and will help create more relaxed looks as well as dressy ones.

Sporty things and elements in the form of elastic bands and zippers are not bad, but they're not suitable for the role of versatile pieces. Don't forget that we do not duplicate the bottoms, neither by color nor by type. For example, you might have one pair of blue straight jeans, one pair of floor-length wide pants in black color, and one satin skirt.

Category #3: Casual top

These are knit tops such as T-shirts. Let your capsule include two T-shirts: one dark and one light. Choose within your range of contrast. For some it will be black and white, and for others it will be navy and beige. It's practical to have dark and light to create monochromatic looks, or vice versa, to create contrasting combinations. They should be of high quality and semi-fitted. Instead of T-shirts, you can use other tops that are not tight fitting. Necklines depend on your body type.

#3.1: Knitted long-sleeve shirts. They are not mandatory, but why not? These can be in dark and light colors too.

Category #4: Formal top

This should be a basic shirt in light shades. Just like the items listed under #2 were a more formal alternative to jeans, this shirt is a more formal alternative to a T-shirt. The shirt is a versatile item. It can work in any outfit from casual to festive and even as a second layer. It can be white, but it doesn't have to be.

#4.1: Dressy top. This is not a must-have item. If you have a cool shirt, it can really dress you up. But if you want, get yourself a second satin fabric shirt or top. The most practical top will be one with wide straps, as it does not require a special bra, unlike tops with thin straps. Tops made of satin fabrics can create beautiful outfits, both casual and evening. The main rule is to choose fabrics that are not transparent. If you don't like silk, satin, or any other satinized fabrics, choose a sewn top or a second shirt made of a dense, smooth fabric.

Category #5: Suit

It is better to buy a suit all at once – then you will have purchased the pants listed under #2. Do not try to buy one suit for all occasions. It is better to divide suits into winter and summer, because they will be different in fabric and color. It is important that the jacket has a lining, is not tight fitting, and sits well on your figure. If you want to wear suits for parties, pay attention to how it fastens and sits on you without the first layer (for evening outings, suits are often worn on the naked body).

Category #6: Casual shoes

We need three pairs of shoes, and they should cover all wardrobe situations. For casual contexts: sneakers, Keds, Uggs, hikers, rough boots like Dr Martins, rough sandals.

Category #7: Closed shoes for more formal outings

Depending on the season, these can be oxfords, loafers, ankle boots, boots, Chelsea boots, or ballet flats.

Category #8: Shoes for evening outings

These can be elegant sandals, kitten heels, boots, ankle boots, ballet flats, or Mary Janes.

Category #9: Bags for casual situations

These are bags for things like shopping. Usually it's big – a backpack or a shopper.

Category #10 Your main bag for weekday looks

The size and type of bag depends on your style. For more masculine looks, choose bags with rigid geometry; for more relaxed looks, you can choose bags made of soft fabric. The main requirement is a minimum of decoration, matte finish, and quality.

Category #11 Small handbag for parties

Some people manage with two handbags: the main one and one for evening outings. Small handbags can be whatever you want – you can play around. And if you want something once and forever, then choose a laconic clutch.

What else?

For demi-season and winter, consider these categories:

Category #12: Basic knitwear

In winter, this is a turtleneck or jumper. You can have one turtleneck and one semi-fitted jumper.

Category #13: A voluminous sweater or sweatshirt

These pieces work well in feminine, minimalist, and relaxed wardrobes. If your dress code is not very strict, then you can wear it to work. The more relaxed the style of your capsule, the more textured your sweater can be, such as a fisherman's sweater. If you are drawn to minimalism or femininity, then I suggest a smooth knit.

An alternative to a voluminous sweater can be a sweatshirt. It is better if it is without a hood and without an elastic band at the waist. Let it be versatile and a real alternative to a sweater – in this case, it will work well in different combinations.

Category #14: A second layer in the form of a cardigan or top shirt

This is an alternative to a jacket to create more cozy and relaxed looks. The shirt can be made of denim, tweed, or leather.

Category #15: One piece

If you don't like the idea of having a suit as a dressy outfit, then you can have a laconic dress – the kind of dress that will easily collaborate with both sneakers and loafers, both a sports bag and a clutch. Such a dress will work as a magic wand. It helps you get quickly ready for any event. It can be a simple cut dress; it could also be a jumpsuit or even a linen dress.

Category #16: Items for relaxed capsules

What is more relaxed than jeans? Of course, a knit suit or a wool dress – casual pieces made of wool, denim, or chunky knitwear.

Category #17 Outerwear

The most neutral and versatile pieces are a midi coat and a trench coat. You can get by with these two items. If your soul requires something more relaxed, then the choice is huge, and it all depends on your preferences. It can be a down coat, a bomber, a biker jacket, a parka, or a fur coat.

Please don't read this list as "This is a must have for every woman's closet." I hope you understand the logic behind the capsule system and can apply it to your own situation.

Notes

Seventeen

Shopping list

H ere's what we've already done:

We have the list of our dressing situations.

We've created our wardrobe structure based on those situations.

We've organized our finalists into capsules.

What should we do next?

Take the shopping list attached below and cross off everything you don't like to wear. I, for example, don't wear fur coats, even if they are faux fur. Others might not like turtlenecks, so they should cross off that item.

Then cross off whatever you already own and are happy with – in other words, cross off your finalists.

Mark clothes on your shopping list that you want to have. Start with items that will fill holes in your capsule backbone.

Then analyze and mark what's missing in the capsule for accents or conceptuality. These can be items from your wish list.

Once you've done these things, you'll have your first, simple, handwritten shopping list.

You can do it now if you want – I'll wait.

Shopping List

Item	How Many	Comments
Top		
T Shirt		
Polo		
Shirt		
Blouse		
Turtleneck		
Sweater		
Skirt		
Pants		
Jeans		
Shorts		
Sundress		
Casual Dress		
Cocktail Dress		

Shopping List

Item	How Many	Comments
Waistcoat		
Jacket		
Cardigan		
Pantsuit		
Bomber		
Denim Jacket		
Biker Jacket		
Trench		
Parka		
Short coat		
Coat		
Down jacket		
Fur Coat		
Sandals		

Shopping List

Item	How Many	Comments
Pointed Toe Ballet Shoes		
Shoes (Mary Jane, Oxfords ect)		
Loafers		
Sneakers or Keds		
Booties		
Ankle Boots		
Boots		
High Boots or Jackboots		
Shopper bag		
Crossbody Bag		
Bag for work		
Clutch		

Shopping List

Item	How Many	Comments
Backpack		
Belt		
Shawl		
Scarf		
Hat		
Fedora Hat		
Earings		
Bracelets		
Necklace		
Ring		
Other		
Other		
Other		
Other		

My Final Shopping List

Now you'll need to make the second shopping list, which is a visual representation of the handwritten one.

We need a visual sheet. Why? Let's say you're discussing the furnishing of your living room with a designer. It's not like he's handing you a list of furniture. He shows catalogs with photos of furniture, and a simple viewing of catalogs isn't enough for you, so you go to see and feel this furniture in person. Our clothes deserve the same respectful, long-forgotten treatment. A visual list is a big money saver. When you're compiling your capsule digitally, you may notice that certain items don't coordinate with each other. You can replace one bag with another without spending any money. You will also see if your capsule is boring or not.

In order to create your visual list, place the photos of the finalists next to the photos of the desired clothes. You can use any editor for this; if you want, you can even draw the capsule on paper or glue photos cut from magazines. You don't have to buy exactly the items you find. It's the concept that matters here. For example, you decide you need a white bag for work and white jeans, so you find a picture of straight white jeans, put them next to the photos of the finalists in the capsule, and see if they match or not. You don't have to buy those jeans, although if you are familiar with the brand, why not?

Check the resulting capsule with sets. You need to create as many sets as possible. Make sure that all the items can be combined, and that the images have the effects and mood you want to translate. In the process, you can adjust the capsule until you are completely satisfied with the result.

Once you have a visual representation of the capsule, you played enough with it, you remove the photos of the finalists. You will be left with the items you need to purchase. This is your final shopping list that you should never deviate from.

To encourage you in this endeavor, here's my definition of what it means to be stylish.

Your unique style is a deeply thought out, carefully prepared carelessness. It's when you oversleep, put on the first thing you see, and drive your toddler to school. You are without makeup, but your eyes shine and your skin looks great – your look in this "first thing you see" is very harmonious. And it's all because you've been thinking long before this ill-fated morning about the color palette, and the silhouettes, and the situations you might find yourself in. That's because you're the director and the costume director of a series titled "My Life."

The next time you go shopping, you won't buy an extra pair of jeans, a pair of sweaters, or a bag because of the cool price. This time, you're going for the things you really need!

That's the way to declutter your closet! Trust me. When you understand your wardrobe you gain confidence. Your attachment to "pity to throw" will gradually fade away.

For those who are completely lost, here is a wonderful template to help you get started (I named it "Student Capsule"). Read this table vertically, horizontally, and diagonally. You will see the work of a well-coordinated team. Insert your own drawings following the same logic.

You are not obligated to use the template. You can make your own in any editor you like.

During the shopping (fitting) process, I recommend testing all your purchases and planned combinations on yourself. It may turn out that you are not very comfortable in some sets or colors – then you can make some adjustments, or you can choose the winner from several candidates.

Are you ready with the shopping list? I'm so happy for you! Congratulations!

7 ITEMS CAPSULE

JUST LIKE SUDOKU

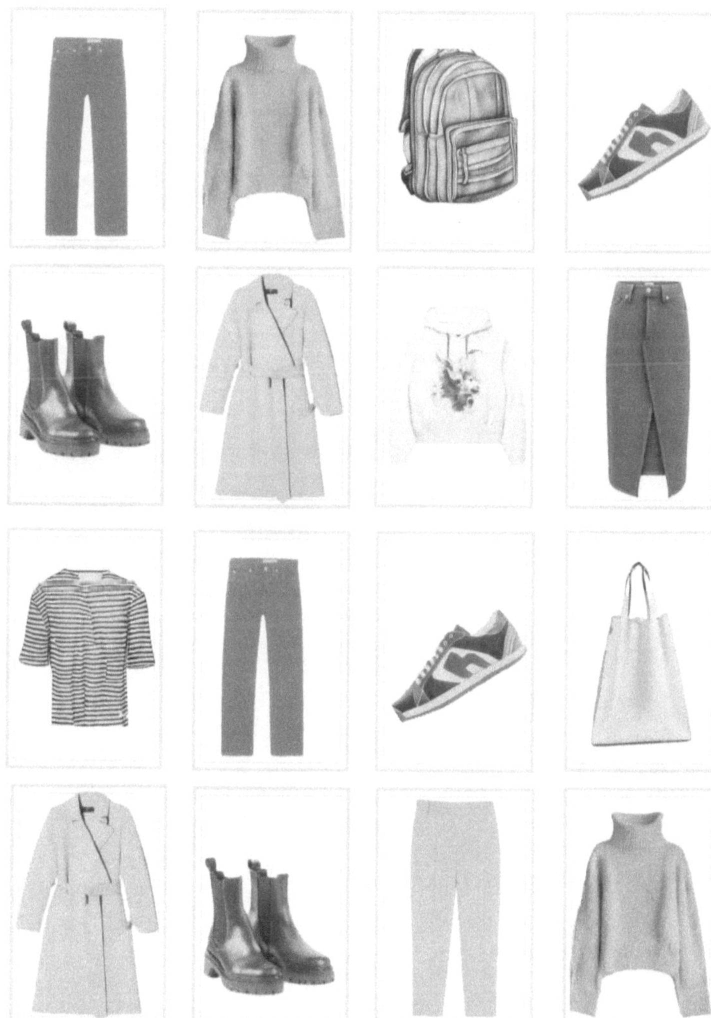

7 ITEMS CAPSULE

JUST LIKE SUDOKU

Draw your capsule here

Eighteen

Example

Here is an extract from my book *The Perfect Summer Capsule,* I think it is a good demonstration of how a capsule should work. It is a bit more complicated, because the backbone consists of four sets and two one-pieces. One can live using the five items on the first picture (one formal set, one relaxed set and one evening dress). I added five more items.

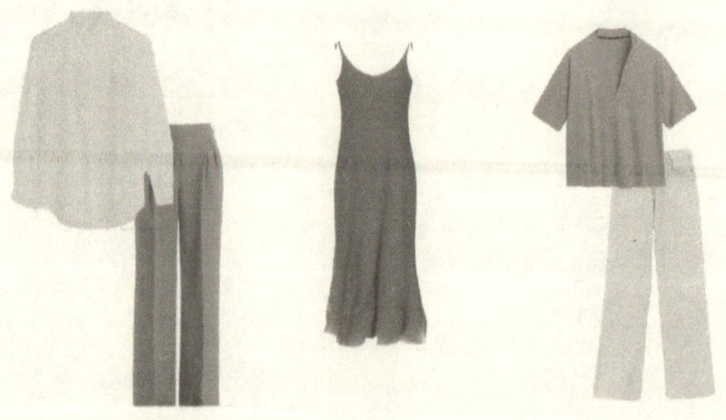

My first "two suits and one dress"

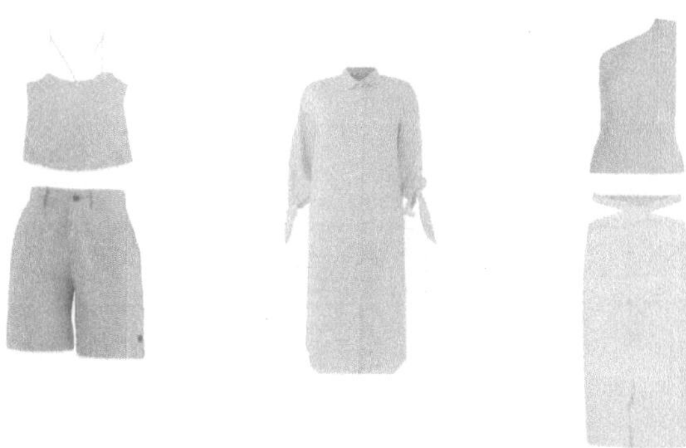

My second "two suits and one dress"

I added two non-basic items – the pink skirt and the blue top. Yes, they are not basic, but they are not very capricious, and they collaborate with other members of the capsule quite well.

You must have noticed that only one of the outfits is business. The ratio may be changed according to your lifestyle.

The second layer.

We are playing only with a basic wardrobe without any difficult team players, so we may have the second layer of basic cut, which will work perfectly with every item.

Second layer

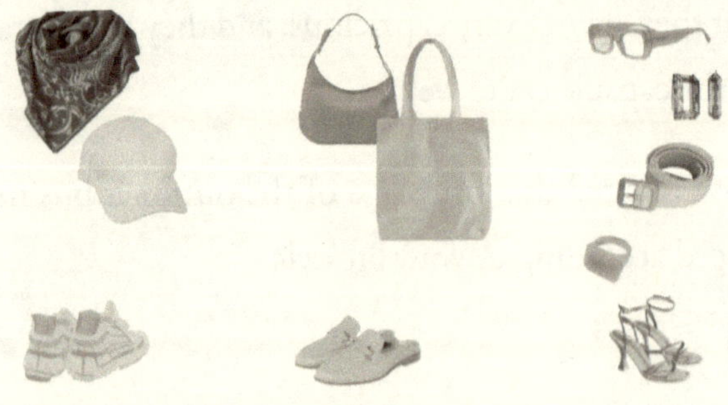

Accessories

I would like to draw your attention to the following. At least two pieces of clothes talk to each other in many outfits shown below. The topic of their conversation may be a color or a common character.

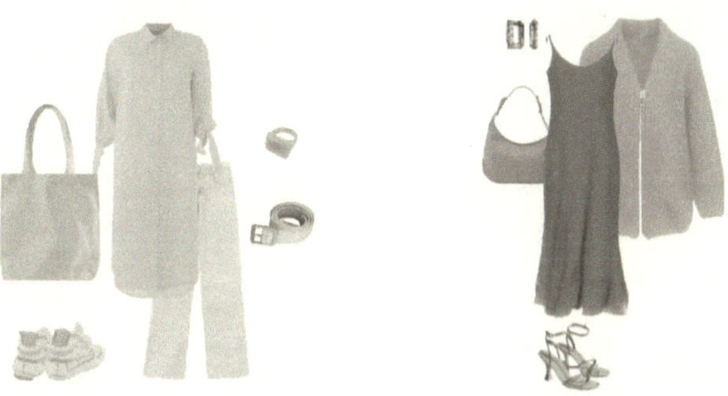

There are no doubles or extras in this capsule.

What can we say about the person who wears this capsule?

She is not afraid of colors, she is a city girl, she goes to the office two or three times a week, but 70% of her wardrobe is casual (her situations might be: walking in the park, going to cafes, parties, city events, shopping or running small errands). She can easily dress up or down for every situation in her life.

I showed several outfits, and I used every item in the capsule, I'll stop here.
I hope you understand that dozens of other interesting combinations can
be created.

Many of you will say: "Oh, no. this capsule is not for me." I would agree
with you. My goal is to inspire you to create your own perfect summer
capsule following the logic.

Nineteen

On importance of Footwear and Bags

I decided to include an extract from my first book *Let's Shop in our own Closet.* I think it is very important to show you this example.

Real-life experience of a young woman

She wakes up in a good mood. That's because there's a regular day ahead, but she is ready for it! The lunch box for her son's school is bought. The shirt is ironed. And breakfast is just as delightful as the mistress of the day.

So, what's the plan? Take her son to school, then go grocery shopping, stop by the post office, and go to the bank.

Here goes.

A nice adventure happened by the school. She saw Him again!

"With whom?"

"Alone with his daughter again. Why is he always alone? Where's his wife? Maybe he's divorced, just like I am?"

She walks her son to the school grounds as if accompanied by drums. That's her heart reacting to Him in a primeval rhythm. And the ripples up the spine...

"Calm down. Breathe slowly. Now, for the groceries and the post office."

She was walking dashingly to the post office along the line of parked cars, when one of the car doors opened and He stepped out. He was nervous as he addressed her.

"Excuse me, I often see you with your son and... I wanted to ask you, do you think you could go out with me today? This afternoon? Maybe we could have some coffee?"

The world stopped. She is just sitting there looking at the sky... How long has it been since she's seen Him? A half an hour, an hour? She is just fine sitting like that for the rest of her life. But the phone yelps, *Bank appointment*. Good Lord! The appointment is in fifteen minutes. Alright, time to run. Put up the hair, change the bag and sneakers. She can do her makeup at the bank.

The line was still huge, even though she had an appointment. Any other time, she'd be annoyed, but not today. She got the loan too. Hurray! Got to run again. What if He hates waiting? She changes the bag and shoes again. She should take the scrunchie out of her hair. A bit of perfume... Well, here goes! She won't get any prettier.

The date was great. But the day's not over yet. There is a long-awaited concert this evening. The babysitter holds the doorbell button forever. She runs to open the door with shining eyes. Here is her evening outfit.

Let's not forget that a shirt is a transformer. If we're going to a business meeting, the shirt is buttoned all the way and is hanging loose. All the lines are crisp and focused. On the other hand, if we're going on a date, we can tuck it in half-way, unbutton a few buttons and pull the neck out to the shoulders or roll up the sleeves.

I think this is one of the most important examples. Of course, this is not a capsule.

Using a trivial set (a white shirt and jeans) as an example, I showed you all four domains (casual, semi-business, romantic, and semi-formal). See the role that accessories play; often, it is they that set the tone.

When you make up a look, you can start with a certain item. For example, you can take a dress and pick out accessories for it. But if you're a fan of basic clothes, it is accessories that help you create the right look.

Remember how we talked about global fashion trends and how pathos and drama are disappearing? The same kind of transformation is taking place in evening-wear. Actually, any routine look can be made into a semi-formal one these days. There is a very practical philosophy behind it: you're at work all day long and you go out at night. Going home where you can style your hair and change into something ornate is a waste of time and effort.

You need universal clothes for quick transformations. They may include midi skirts and pleated skirts, laconic mini skirts and dresses, culottes, jackets, shirts, any office outfit, lingerie-style clothes or satiny ones. If we talk about fabrics, then leather, denim, tweed, suit fabrics and satiny fabrics are very good transformers from a day-job to evening-out. Linen and knitwear, however, are much worse at it or they can't transform at all. All of the above clothes are basic.

What conclusion can we draw from this? Get yourself an accessory base that includes a pair of semi-formal shoes, a purse (anything small, not necessarily a clutch-purse), and a couple of fashion accessories and that's it.

Twenty

Lifehacks and Farewell

How to organize your closet

A very common question is whether you need to separate capsules in your closet, and the answer is no. It's more of a notional structural division for your understanding. Plus, if you have items that are versatile, then even in a complex wardrobe, they will "live" in several capsules at once and mix with different pieces. That's why I don't recommend separating capsules physically in your closet.

A better way to organize your closet is by functional positions (bottoms, shirts, knitwear, second layers). Put them in the order in which you are accustomed to assembling sets – usually we start with bottoms or one-pieces, then choose a top and a second layer, and then we finish our outfit with an accessory set (shoes, bag, jewelry) and outerwear.

We put away non-seasonal garments after sorting out the closet. Where? Either upstairs, downstairs, or somewhere else. Why? So that we always have only usable items in active access.

Daily planner: "What I Wore"

I want to share with you one more unscientific method – or maybe it actually is scientific. It's about how to weed out ineffective doubles from the closet by the method of elimination and identify a strong backbone. Maybe you can use it.

At the beginning of the season, start a separate experimental rail outside your closet or inside your dressing room, where a strong core of items for the season (your most-used base plus a couple of most-used accents) will end up.

How do you do this? Start wearing what you have, and the ones you wear most often are relegated to that rail. That way, by mid-season, you will be able to:

Identify the strongest base and the strongest accents.

See which doubles are the weakest, and in good conscience remove them from your closet altogether.

Figure out which pieces you generally feel more comfortable wearing and what to bet on in future seasons when planning your purchases. When you make your next shopping list, you will pay more attention to pants, for example, and the purchase of a skirt will be left with the comment "if there is money and desire."

It takes time to track yourself. To be honest, one or two weeks is not quite enough. I've developed a daily planner called "What I Wore" that you can find on Amazon. It's a regular planner that allows you to plan your days, and it has the added feature that every day you can log what you wore and track your mood. If you'd like to use it, I invite you to do so.

Buffer zone

For those who find it very difficult to part with clothes, I advise doing it through the "buffer zone." This is a box with outsiders and used items that are difficult for you to part with. It is needed so that you can safely do seasonal cleaning, but to give yourself more comfort, you can send these items to the buffer instead of throwing them straight away. If you never once turned to these garments during the season, then you definitely didn't need them, and you can finally remove them from your closet.

Remember those NO and QUESTIONABLE boxes? Well, if you still have doubts about something, send it to the buffer for a year. And then don't forget to free it up once a year for new outsiders.

Photograph successful finds

Take photos of successful combinations, print them out, and stick them on the back of the closet doors. If you need to get dressed in a hurry, you'll have a clue. By the way, compare your new outfits with the ones you made at the beginning of this book. Do you notice any changes?

And that's really all I have on this one – I've tried to be concise. It has been my pleasure to share with you all the techniques of capsule construction, and I really hope that you will be able to build the capsule of your dreams and manage it cleverly. The most important thing is never to forget that we manage our clothes, they don't manage us!

With love, A

***

I invite you to read *I Will Dress Any Body Type*. It will bring you to a whole different level in your sartorial development!

***

Would you like to see more Capsules, download your free gift, "Capsule Ideas"(www.alayaaifel.com). Get inspired! Thank you again for reading this book!